Tynemouth Priory and Castle

Grace McCombie

C000284850

Introduction

The dramatic headland at Tynemouth is a natural fortress commanding the entrance to the river Tyne, the gateway to Newcastle. Connected to the mainland only by a narrow neck of rock and defined by tall cliffs, Tynemouth headland was virtually unassailable before the development of modern guns and has been occupied intermittently, as both a stronghold and a place of worship, for more than 2,000 years.

Remains of an Iron Age settlement have been discovered here but the first written record of occupation dates from the eighth century, when a monastic community was established. Its wooden buildings were destroyed during the Viking invasions of the ninth and tenth centuries. The medieval ruins visible today belong to a second monastery, Tynemouth Priory, founded in the late 11th century and dedicated to St Oswine (d.651), whose body was preserved here in a rich shrine. King Henry VIII suppressed the priory in 1539 but the church nave remained in parish use until the late 17th century.

Because of its strategic value in protecting the mouth of the Tyne, the headland was fortified until the 1950s. A gatehouse, which still exists, was built as part of the defence in the 14th century. Over the centuries, the defences were adapted and added to – a barracks, governor's house and a spectacular lighthouse were all built in the 17th century. These later buildings have now gone, although 19th- and 20th-century gun emplacements remain, a lasting reminder of the military importance of Tynemouth.

Above: *Lance bombardier Bob Jones standing on the platform of Hope House Command Post, looking south across Percy Gardens towards Tynemouth Castle in 1942. The platform was used for cleaning the lenses of the Barr and Stroud rangefinder, which worked with the 9.2-inch gun in the castle*

Facing page: *View of the ruins of Tynemouth Priory from the north*

Tour

FOLLOWING THE TOUR

*The tour begins at the entrance to
the church, continues with a
walk round the fortifications and
ends at the gatehouse.*

The splendid abbey ruins occupy the middle of the
headland. In the Middle Ages the priory church was
the central feature of a large group of monastic
buildings, most of which have disappeared. The
medieval gatehouse stands at the landward neck of
the peninsula, closing the circuit of its natural,
cliff-edged defences. Along the cliffs are the remains
of fortifications dating from the Middle Ages to the
20th century, including gun batteries that guarded
the mouth of the Tyne from the 1880s to the 1950s.

Above: *A view down the length
of the priory church,
looking towards the east end*

❶ PRIORY CHURCH ENTRANCE

The remains of the priory church today largely date from two main building periods: the first, from about 1090 and the second, from about 1190–1210. The main front of the church, an architectural showpiece of the first half of the 13th century, retains its richly detailed central doorway, with the remains of niches to house statues on the right and a damaged window (probably a 14th-century addition) to the left. The broad window over the door was another late medieval alteration. In the lawn to the right of the church front is the low, stone foundation of a tower that was constructed against the west front in the 14th century. It might have been built as a belfry but a survey of 1577 describes it as 'the high prison', which suggests that it served later as a gaol.

❷ THE NAVE AND CROSSING

The church was built to a conventional cross-shaped plan, divided into a number of sections. The western part, or nave, was open to all visitors but the rest of the church was the monks' domain, and outsiders were admitted only by their permission, to visit the shrine of the saint. After the suppression of the monastery in 1538, and until the 17th century, the townspeople of Tynemouth used the nave as their parish church, building a wall to block off the nave from the disused monastic church. This disused part gradually fell into disrepair, but the blocking wall protected the rood screen, the survival of which is today one of Tynemouth's most unusual features. The rood screen is the stone wall, pierced by two doors at the far end of the nave, which marked the division between the nave and the eastern part of the church reserved for the monks. An altar stood against it and a large

PRIORY CHURCH ENTRANCE

❶ Doorway
❷ Niches for statues
❸ Central window opening
❹ Window inserted in 1340s
❺ Foundations of tower, originally possibly a belfry but later used as a prison

image of Christ on the cross (or rood), flanked by the figures of St John the Baptist and the Virgin Mary hung above it.

When first laid out in about 1090 the nave was much shorter than at present but it already had the standard form of a tall central space flanked by lower vaulted aisles. A single bay of the north aisle remains intact, with its arches blocked, to one side of the rood screen; it was partitioned off when the parish took the nave over as its church after its suppression, probably to create a vestry. It now contains large stone sarcophagi excavated from the site.

In about 1240 the nave was extended westward; the junction between the old and new work is visible in the masonry of the walls and the changing form of the arcade bases in the ground. The wall running across the nave, of which only the foundation survives, was probably built when the church was reorganized as a military storehouse in the 17th century. Visible against the left (north) wall of the church are fragments of medieval ceramic and stone paving.

■ CHOIR AND PRESBYTERY

The monks' domain lay beyond the rood screen. The transept – the short arms of the church running north-south – meets the main axis at the crossing. Around this are the remains of four massive piers which supported the central tower. Immediately to the east of this was the choir screen, which has disappeared. This made the crossing into an intermediate space between the laity in the nave and the sacred enclosure of the choir and presbytery. The latter was the heart of the monastery, the space where the monks gathered together for their devotions, sitting in stalls which faced each other next to the crossing. Raised on a platform at the far end, in the area still enclosed on two sides by high walls, was the high altar. Beyond this stood the shrine of St Oswine beneath a splendid silver cover decorated with gold and jewels.

NAVE AND CROSSING

1 Stone rood screen, dividing the nave and the crossing

2 The rough masonry above the rood screen was added to make the east end wall of the parish church which was made out of the priory nave after the monastery was suppressed in 1539

3 Only surviving bay of the 1090s church. It was partitioned off when it became a parish church

4 Crossing piers

The choir and presbytery were rebuilt in about 1190. The foundations of the 11th-century choir were discovered during excavations in 1905 and are marked out in concrete in the grass. It had a round east end encircled by an aisle or ambulatory with three small, semi-circular chapels projecting from it. This type of plan was common in contemporary Benedictine churches of the 11th century in both France and England.

The new east end seems to have been built in two stages, perhaps to allow the old Norman choir to remain in use during its construction. The easternmost three bays of the sanctuary which housed St Oswine's shrine, with tall lancet windows still standing to their full height, were probably built first. The aisled choir was probably built once the Norman choir was demolished.

The culmination was the tiered lancets of the end wall, similar to the east windows of contemporary buildings at Whitby Abbey in Yorkshire, and the Nine Altars Chapel at Durham Cathedral. The presbytery was vaulted in stone, presumably to signal the importance of the shrine of St Oswine, whereas the rest of the church may have had flat or barrel-vaulted timber ceilings. Even in its ruined state, it is one of the great Gothic monuments of northern England.

Above: Reconstruction drawing of the choir and presbytery in about 1300. The monks stand in stalls on either side of the choir. To the east is the high altar and beyond is the shrine of St Oswine

Below: A monk praying before a shrine (detail), from the Lives of Saints Edmund and Fremund, (1434–44)

The high altar and St Oswine's shrine probably stood towards the east end of the presbytery. Even now its surviving walls are superbly articulated with richly carved window openings and blind arcading. In the wall to the right (south) are five niches at ground level. From right to left these were probably two seats for priests officiating at the Mass; a water basin called a piscina for washing the altar vessels; a cupboard for storing books and valuables; and a broad niche for a tomb. An identical tomb niche stands in the opposite wall: in such positions so close to the shrine, they were presumably created for powerful patrons.

The broad arch in the east wall, now with a door, was probably a recess for an altar. In the 15th century this was converted into the entrance to the so-called Percy chantry. The stumps of vaulting are clearly visible high in the walls of the shrine – the only part of the church that had high-level masonry vaults.

In the 1340s it is recorded that St Oswine's shrine was moved into a more spacious setting so that pilgrims could visit it without disturbing services at the altar. This could mean that it was moved out of the presbytery and taken to the Lady Chapel, which was at the north-east of the church.

It was probably at about the same time that an extra floor was created above the presbytery vault: remains of its windows can be seen high up on the south and east walls. It was reached by a system of stairs and passages threaded through the walls. The purpose of the extra floor is not clear: a similar feature at nearby Brinkburn Priory is thought to have been built to provide extra accommodation; another at Lindisfarne was apparently connected with the fortification of the church. At Tynemouth the upper chamber might have been used by the guardians of a fire that was kept burning to guide mariners. In 1582 there was an order to restore a light in the east end of the church 'as in former times had been'.

4 THE PERCY CHANTRY

The small door at the end of the presbytery leads into an exquisitely decorated late 15th-century chantry – a chapel where Mass would be chanted for the person or family who endowed it. The chapel was known mistakenly as the Lady Chapel, or St Mary's chapel – the real Lady Chapel lay to the north – until, in 1907, the historian H H E Craster suggested that it should be called the Percy Chapel because the arms and emblems of this powerful northern family appear in its decoration (see feature opposite). Although it has been known by this name ever since, the patron of the chapel was more likely to have been Prior John Langton (c.1450–78), whose initials I L P (Iohannes Langton Prior) appear twice in the ceiling. If so, the chapel was probably built after the Percy family was restored to the earldom of Northumberland in 1471 and before Langton's death in 1478.

**SOUTH WALL OF
THE PRESBYTERY**

1 Two seats for priests

2 A water basin for washing altar vessels

3 A cupboard for storing books and objects used in the Mass

4 A recess for the tomb

Percy Chantry

The 15th-century Percy Chantry is the only part of the priory church to survive complete, although it is much restored. The low heavy vaulting is composed of ingeniously intersecting ribs with carved bosses. A key to the subjects contained on the bosses is given below.

1 Eagle of St John, holding scroll (broken)
2 Head of Christ
3 Angel of St Matthew, holding scroll
4 IHS under a crown
5 Square rose
6 St John the Evangelist seated, holding palm leaf and book
7 Risen Christ, holding banner, with figure of Mary Magdalene below
8 St James the Less seated, holding fuller's bat and book
9 M, the monogram of the Virgin
10 Emblems of the Crucifixion – crown of thorns, cross, three nails and hammer
11 St Philip seated, holding three leaves and book

12 St Andrew seated
13 St Thomas seated, holding book and spear
14 Star with nine rays
15 Circular rose
16 St Paul seated, holding sword and book, with a head under a cushion at his feet
17 Christ seated between four angels and trumpets
18 St Peter seated, holding keys and book, with a head under a cushion at his feet
19 Sun encircled by IHVS MERCY
20 Bearded head
21 St Bartholomew seated, holding book and flaying knife
22 St James seated, holding staff and book

23 St Matthew seated, holding book and saw
24 Percy crescent and fetterlock on shield
25 Monograms of Prior John Langton
26 St Symeon seated, holding book and pillar
27 St John the Baptist, holding a lamb
28 St Thaddeus seated, holding book and halberd
29 Monogram of Prior John Langton
30 Emblems of the five wounds of Christ
31 Lion of St Mark, holding scroll
32 Lamb of God with cross and flag
33 Ox of St Luke, holding scroll

Above: Lady Chapels were often decorated splendidly and provided with musical instruments such as organs to accompany the monks' singing. This marginal illustration is from a book of hours 1310–20
Right: Only the foundation of the south wall of the lady chapel survives. Built to the north of the presbytery in the 1330s, it was more than 21 metres (70ft) long

It was repaired for use after the parish abandoned the priory nave for a new church in North Shields by the 1660s: it was a convenient place to hold funeral services for those who were buried on the headland. In about 1810 it was converted into a magazine for storing ammunition. John Dobson (1787–1865), an architect whose work includes Newcastle's Central Station as well as the 1858 restoration of Hexham Abbey, restored the chapel in 1850. He covered the floor with Minton tiles and restored the roof bosses. A small stone altar was set at the east end and a starry sky painted on the vault. From 1878 to 1879 further restoration work was done: all the stained glass was repaired by the Newcastle manufactory of William Wailes (1808–81), the windows were rehung, and a new window inserted to the memory of William Sydney Gibson (d.1871), historian of the priory.

⑤ EAST END EXTERIOR AND LADY CHAPEL

Leaving the Percy Chantry and turning to the right outside the church ruins, the visitor passes the site of the Lady Chapel. There was a strong tradition of monastic devotion to the Virgin Mary and so-called Lady Chapels, dedicated to her, were often splendidly decorated and provided in the later Middle Ages with instruments such as organs to accompany music sung in them. This chapel, described as 'new' in 1336, was connected to the presbytery. It was a sumptuous building standing more than 21m (70ft) long and projecting eastwards beyond the line of the Percy

Chantry. Demolished after the suppression, only the foundation of its south wall survives, but the line of its roof can be seen on the outside wall of the presbytery.

The exterior of the presbytery was almost as richly detailed as the interior. Visible in the masonry of the east wall is the A-shaped outline of the steeply pitched 13th-century roof gable. This was overbuilt, probably in the 14th century, when the church was raised by one storey. The great height of the east wall made it a landmark for sailors.

6 CLOISTER AND CHAPTER HOUSE

On the south side of the church are the remains of the monastic buildings. At Tynemouth, these seem to have followed the standard layout in part, with the chapter house on the east side, the monks' dormitory on the upper floor of the east wing, the refectory on the south side, and cellars and storage in the west wing. The remains are fragmentary, though, and were badly damaged by the construction of a massive vaulted magazine in the middle of the cloister area in the 19th century (see photograph on page 38).

The chapter house retains enough evidence of its design, with shaft bases flanking its doorway and remains of stone benches and decorative blind arcading on its north wall, to suggest that it was rebuilt in the mid- to late 13th century.

The chapter house was so-called because it was where the monks met every day, beginning their meetings with the reading of a chapter of the rule of St Benedict. The plan of the cloister is marked out in the lawn to the south of the

Left: A chapter house, from a Flemish manuscript, first half of the 15th century. Sitting on stone benches round the side of the room, the monks would gather here every day to hear a chapter of the rule, to discuss business and to pardon or punish members of the community

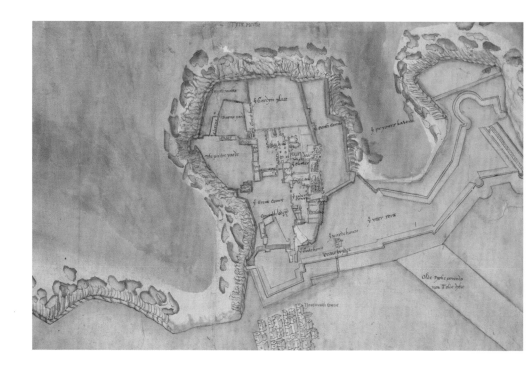

Above: A survey of 1582 showing buildings on the headland, now gone. These buildings probably date back to monastic times, but do not necessarily represent the monastic layout, as the survey was made 40 years after the monastery was suppressed in 1539. Nonetheless, it shows that the headland housed a large and largely self-sufficient community. Note the large yard to the left (north) of the church with stables, barn, cow house, poultry and barnyards. The house adjoining the church might have been the priest's house, from the time when the priory church was converted to parish use. To the right (south) of the great court is an inner court, west of the cloister buildings, with brewhouse, bakehouse, mill, malthouse, and lodgings around it

nave. The two doors into the church in its north-east corner gave the monks access to both presbytery and nave.

7 DORMITORY, PRIOR'S CHAMBERS

Next to the chapter house the base of a ruined stair opens onto the cloister walk. This rose to a dormitory that extended towards the cliff along the upper floor of the east range. The dormitory was under construction in 1111 and was extended southward in the 13th century.

The uses of the various rooms beneath the dormitory are uncertain and their arrangement has changed through time. One interior containing the remains of a late medieval tile floor was possibly the warming room, the only place in the monastery other than the kitchens that had a fireplace.

Beyond it is a cluster of ruins, most dating from the 13th century. To the south are the remains of an impressive suite of rooms, ending in a high wall with two blocked windows. Next to this is a small but finely detailed room which retains its original vaulted ceiling. It is possible that these were the prior's chambers. They could have supported fine rooms at first-floor level, including possibly the prior's private chapel, but the question of these buildings' original use is unlikely to be answered definitively.

8 LATRINES AND INFIRMARY

To the east are the remains of the monastic latrines. These were situated on the upper floor and directly accessible from the dormitory. Waste from them was flushed by a piped water supply and drained to the cliffs below. Just beyond the latrine are walls that possibly belonged to the monastic

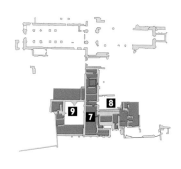

infirmary. They and the fortifications in this area were destroyed when the approaches to the present north pier were made in the later 19th century. All the buildings against the cliff were heavily buttressed against the slope.

◙ REFECTORY AND NEW HALL

To the west of the possible prior's lodgings is a long late 13th-century building that the 1582 survey labels the New Hall: again, we are not sure of its original function, but this may have been the priory's guest house.

Of the other cloister buildings, fewer traces remain. South of the cloister (and north of the 'New Hall' shown in the 1582 survey) was the refectory, where the monks ate. Only two walls of this building now remain. Meals were eaten in silence to the accompaniment of devotional readings. The pulpit from which these were read was probably supported on the triangular base visible in the ground. Beside the refectory was a kitchen, the site of which is identified by the surviving base of a round oven.

Only fragments of the west range of the cloister survive: there is some evidence of the room adjoining the west end of the church, with a blocked doorway, remains of a decorative arcade and the outline of a vaulted external porch. This might have been the parlour, where monks could entertain visitors, but again, we cannot be certain. In a standard monastic plan, the rest of the vanished west range would have been used for storage.

Left: Only the south and east walls of the refectory at Tynemouth remain. The monks ate in silence while being read to from a pulpit, not unlike the arrangement shown in this 15th-century Flemish manuscript

Exiled to Tynemouth

'Day and night the waves break and roar and undermine the cliff. Thick sea frets roll in wrapping everything in gloom. Dim eyes, hoarse voices, sore throats are the consequence'

From the 13th century, the abbots of St Albans sent recalcitrant monks to Tynemouth as a punishment. It is possible that one such exile wrote the first known description of the priory in the form of a letter written in Latin which paints a vivid picture of life here in deliberately colourful prose. Nothing is known about its date of composition or authorship but a reference to the completion of the new church suggests a date in the 1340s.

'Our house is confined to the top of a high rock and is surrounded by sea on every side but one. Here is the approach to the monastery through a gate cut out of the rock so narrow that a cart can hardly pass through. Day and night the waves break and roar and undermine the cliff. Thick sea frets roll in wrapping everything in gloom. Dim eyes, hoarse voices, sore throats are the consequence ... Shipwrecks are frequent. It is a great pity to see the numbed crew, whom no power on earth can save, whose vessel, mast swaying and timbers parted, rushes upon the rock or reef. No ringdove or nightingale is here, only grey birds which nest in rocks and greedily prey upon the drowned, whose screaming cry is a token of a coming storm ... In the Spring the sea air blights the blossoms of the stunted fruit trees, so that you are lucky to find a wizened apple, though it will set your teeth on edge if you try to eat it. See to it, dear brother, that you do not come to this comfortless place. But the church is of wondrous beauty. It has been lately completed. Within it rests the body of the blessed martyr, Oswine, in a silver shrine, magnificently decorated with gold and jewels. He protects the murderers, thieves and seditious persons who fly to him and commutes their punishment to exile. He heals those whom no doctor can cure. The martyr's protection and the church's beauty furnish us with a bond of unity. We are well off for food, thanks to the abundant supply of fish of which we tire.'

Below: Monks were sent to Tynemouth as a punishment in the 13th century. Here a monk and a woman are put in the stocks. From an illustration in the Smithfield Decretals, *c.1340*

Left: 'The Burial of Sir John Moore at La Coruña, 1809', by Thomas Ballard (fl.1865–77). Moore was killed during the withdrawal of the British Army from Spain. A career soldier from Glasgow, he pioneered the creation of light infantry as an effective force and was popular with the ordinary soldier. Corporal Alexander Rollo, who holds the lamp, is buried on the headland at Tynemouth. He died in 1856, at the age of 82. The burial was made famous by the Revd Charles Wolfe's poem 'Funeral of Sir John Moore' (1817) which became one of the 19th-century's most celebrated poems in the English language
Below: The Monk Stone, in the graveyard south of the presbytery was brought here in 1935. It is the base of a ninth-century cross shaft and was reused in the Middle Ages to mark the boundary of the priory's estates

GRAVEYARD

Although the church nave ceased to be a parish church in the mid-17th century, the parish continued to use the area as a burial ground. Most of the gravestones and monuments date to the late 18th and early 19th centuries. Of especial interest is the grave of Corporal Alexander Rollo, who is said to have held the lamp at Sir John Moore's burial after the 1809 battle of Corunna in the Peninsular Wars. Rollo died in 1856, at the age of 82. Another commemorates members of the Wright family including John Wright of Dockwray Square, 'founder of several elegant streets' in North Shields and Newcastle.

It was not easy to reconcile parish use of the headland for burials with the needs of a fortress and eventually, in 1826, the parish agreed to limit burials to existing vaults, and supposedly, no further graves or vaults were dug. The parish had been provided with a new church, Christ Church, in North Shields, west of Tynemouth, which was completed by Robert Trollope in 1668 (enlarged in 1792). Many old graves on the headland at Tynemouth were removed by military operations in the 19th century.

The Monk Stone in the graveyard south of the presbytery was brought here in 1935 from a farm to the north of Tynemouth. It is the base of a ninth-century cross shaft which was perhaps reused in the later Middle Ages to mark the boundary of the priory estates known as the Liberty of Tynemouth. The stone was carved with intricate patterns of foliage, animals and interlacing and a hunting scene seems to have been depicted on the base.

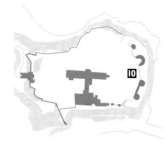

⑩ GUN BATTERIES

Because of their strategic position commanding the approaches to the river mouth, the artillery defences of Tynemouth remained in use between the mid-16th and mid-20th centuries. Like all English coastal defences, they were not always adequately armed, supplied or manned, being made ready or updated only when conflict was imminent. From about 1881, however, Tynemouth was redeveloped as part of a modernized system of coastal defences to protect the Tyne and its approaches. A line of gun positions, constructed between 1891 and 1905, remains at the tip of the headland. These were manned for defence and training until the new science of guided rocketry brought an end to all coastal artillery in the British Army in 1956.

The guns were fixed to the floors of concrete emplacements, masked by earth banks to absorb the force of incoming shells. At the south end overlooking Prior's Haven and the river mouth are two positions for light 12-pounder quick-firing (QF) guns of the early 1900s, designed to fire on fast torpedo boats trying to break into the river. To the north are two emplacements for Mk VII 6-inch guns of 1902 (one now has a later, Mark XXIII 6-inch gun installed) and a third for a Mk X 9.2-inch gun of 1904; all were long-range guns to give protection against armoured warships further out at sea. These guns were protected from aerial attack by concrete gun-houses in the Second World War, faint scars of which can be seen in the floors behind the 9.2-inch emplacement. The northernmost emplacement, now covered over, was built in 1893 for a 6-inch gun on a 'disappearing' mounting. This type used the recoil of the gun, held on long pivoting arms, to retract the barrel into the safety of a deep pit for reloading. The energy of recoil was stored in hydro-pneumatic pistons which, on release, returned the gun to the firing position.

Along the north side of the headland, back towards the gatehouse, an 1859 cannon commemorates the 25th anniversary in 1984 of the First Volunteer Artillery Tynemouth Association.

Right: Tynemouth's gun positions, overlooking the river mouth. In the foreground is a circular emplacement for a 6-inch gun, with its gun detachment shelter and magazine entrance beyond

CUTAWAY RECONSTRUCTION OF THE 6-INCH GUN BATTERY AND MAGAZINES DURING THE FIRST WORLD WAR

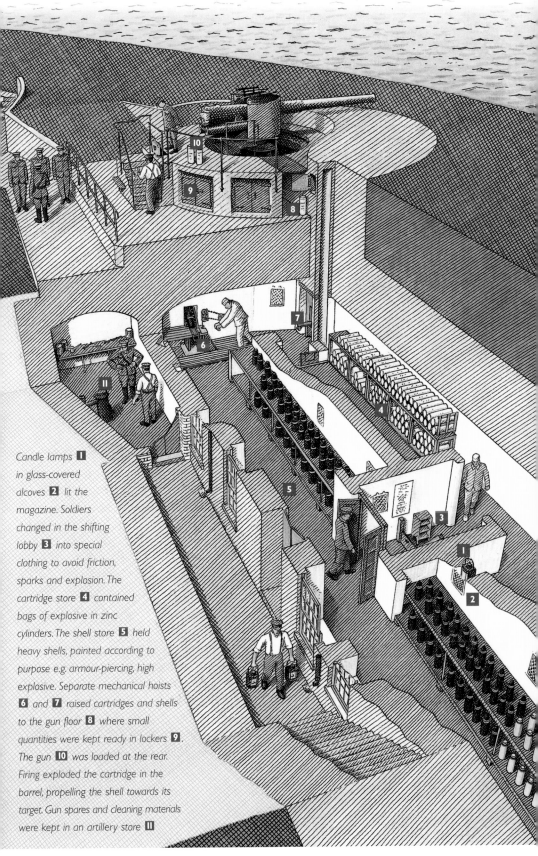

Candle lamps **1** in glass-covered alcoves **2** lit the magazine. Soldiers changed in the shifting lobby **3** into special clothing to avoid friction, sparks and explosion. The cartridge store **4** contained bags of explosive in zinc cylinders. The shell store **5** held heavy shells, painted according to purpose e.g. armour-piercing, high explosive. Separate mechanical hoists **6** and **7** raised cartridges and shells to the gun floor **8** where small quantities were kept ready in lockers **9**. The gun **10** was loaded at the rear. Firing exploded the cartridge in the barrel, propelling the shell towards its target. Gun spares and cleaning materials were kept in an artillery store **11**

Above: Aerial view of the headland at Tynemouth, showing the castle walls hugging the cliff edge. The seaward wall was removed for big gun batteries in the 19th century, the landward wall modified for cannon in the 18th, and the rest adapted for musket and rifle fire in the 18th and 19th centuries. Small sections of medieval castle wall survive around the circuit

Below: The massive Collingwood Monument, 1847, to the south of the headland. Newcastle-born Admiral Collingwood (1748–1810) commanded the fleet after Nelson's death at Trafalgar in 1805. The four guns are from his ship the Royal Sovereign

OUTLYING MODERN DEFENCES

The site's defensive value is most obvious from the south, looking out over the river. No movement of shipping in or out of the river could go unobserved. Just visible at Spanish Battery, on the lower headland adjacent to the car park beyond Prior's Haven, are the partial remains of two 6-inch and two 12-pounder gun emplacements. The guns there and on the headland were only the core of a sophisticated system of which battery observation posts, position-finding cells and searchlights also formed a part; several of these were off the headland and most have been destroyed. South of the priory at the foot of the cliffs was a concrete defence post and guard point to watch for enemy mines being dropped into the river by parachute. Just north of where the North Pier leaves the cliffs, a concrete platform, now railed, is the site of a searchlight. During the Second World War, Park Battery was built on the opposite side of the river at South Shields. In 1940, it was equipped with 6-inch guns, replaced in 1943 by sophisticated 5.25-inch guns that could fire at both ships and aircraft.

FORTRESS WALLS

A massive earth bank forms a key element in the defences at the neck of the headland, facing inland. The medieval gatehouse is set into it, and medieval and later walls were built on it. Though the origin of the bank is unknown, it might have formed part of the defences of an early castle of the Norman period, or perhaps a rampart defending the late Iron Age settlement. It was used and adapted by all the later defences. The surviving walls are a patchwork of many periods. The western walls, across the neck of the headland and to either side of the gatehouse, were always the most

vulnerable part. From the medieval defences, fragments of the curtain walls survive. These probably date from 1296, when King Edward I gave the prior 'licence to crenellate' or fortify the site. The walls enclosed the level summit of the headland, following the irregular cliff edge to make a formidable obstacle. The most complete section of medieval wall includes and runs eastwards from East Mount Tower, descending towards Prior's Haven. This stretch of medieval wall once

Above: Tynemouth Priory from the pier, in about 1895. Note the lighthouse and military buildings on the headland

Below: Tynemouth headland. The surviving stretches of medieval wall are marked in red

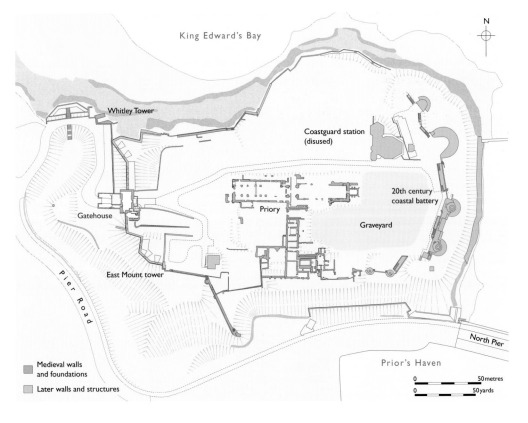

RECONSTRUCTION DRAWING
OF THE GATEHOUSE IN ABOUT 1400

formed an outer enclosure. Most of it was demolished when the road to North Pier was built, and stone quarried, between the 1850s and 1890s.

East Mount Tower retains some medieval fabric but its large splayed embrasure, or opening, was probably made for a cannon in the 16th century. The wall east of it is crenellated, probably adapting the medieval form for muskets and rifles in the 18th and 19th centuries. The medieval defences on either side of the gatehouse were remodelled from the 1540s. The massive earth rampart was faced with masonry possibly in about 1783 when the gatehouse was converted into barracks. The rampart has stone platforms from which cannon could fire towards the land through embrasures in a low, sloping parapet. Inside the rampart long ramps enabled easy movement of the guns.

West of the gatehouse, the triangular earthwork (redan) with its low stone revetment was established in the late 18th century, again probably in 1783. Originally, it was higher, with a parapet for the garrison to defend the gatehouse. Beyond it, the huge ditch is mainly the result of the construction of Pier Road and by quarrying in the 19th century although it is partly on the line of the great ditch dug here from about 1545 on the perimeter of the fortress.

The northern wall dates mainly from the 18th and 19th centuries, built to defend the beach and cliffs with musket and rifle fire both through square, splayed loops and over a low, sloping parapet. There is some medieval fabric, notably at the north-west corner in the cliff beside the road. Here are the remains of the three-storey Whitley Tower, sited to watch the beach below and best seen from the beach today. Most of it has fallen down the cliff and now only its lowest storey remains. The construction of the Victorian gun batteries entirely removed the eastern walls of the castle.

 THE GATEHOUSE

The great gatehouse is the only building of the medieval defences to have survived intact. Begun in 1390, it was the main entrance to the headland. Heavily fortified and conceived on a huge scale, it expresses the wealth and power of the institution it protected with a series of grand rooms. It is not clear who lived there in the Middle Ages but it might have been the residence and courthouse of the administrator of the monastic estate, the so-called Liberty of Tynemouth. A carving of arms reputedly belonging to Prior Robert de Rhodes (ruled c.1440) was once displayed on the gatehouse but was moved to Newcastle in 1705.

The gatehouse lies in the centre of the earth rampart that protects the landward approach to the headland. Its principal tower was once crowned by angle turrets and battlements. This was protected to the front by a fortified courtyard

KEY TO THE GATEHOUSE

1 Barbican
2 Stair turret
3 Wall-walk
4 Angle turrets
5 Hall
6 Great chamber
7 Kitchen
8 Fireplace
9 Oven
10 Drawbridge

called a barbican. To the rear is another much smaller walled enclosure. Any one who got through the outer gate and portcullis would find themselves trapped below the main tower and exposed to fire from above. The vaulted ground-level rooms might have been used as storage spaces and the present shop probably served as a porter's lodge. The upper levels of the gatehouse were reached through a raised doorway which stood level with the ramparts. This entrance was protected by a drawbridge that could be raised flush to the wall within the recessed rectangular panel around it. A modern bridge now spans the drawbridge pit. On the first floor of the gatehouse was a hall, used as a public reception room. Above this and connected to it by a spiral stair was another grand room with large windows. This was probably a great chamber and bedroom, where the chief occupant of the gatehouse could withdraw from company and sleep. The floor level between the two rooms is marked by the lines of projecting stones that supported the timbers in the walls.

Above: The redan, a triangular walled enclosure, was established in about 1783 as an extra defence outside the gatehouse. Today it can be seen as an earthwork (across the centre of the photograph) without its original parapet wall

Below: Tynemouth gatehouse from a drawing of about 1780, before the building was remodelled as a barracks. Compare with the photograph on facing page

Next to the great hall was a small kitchen built up against the tower. Preserved in one wall are a fire, drain and bread oven. Above was a small room of uncertain use that opened into the great chamber. From the great hall there was also access to the barbican wall-walks and chambers.

In 1783 the building was remodelled as a barracks and the barbican was built over. The line of the pitched roof erected at this time is faintly visible in the masonry at the front of the gatehouse. After a fire in 1936, the Ministry of Works stripped away these additions to reveal the walls of the 14th-century gatehouse as they appear today.

In the 14th century several great monasteries, such as Bury St Edmunds and Thornton, erected fortified gatehouses to their precincts. None, however, has such military characteristics as Tynemouth, which is comparable to contemporary castle buildings in the region. In overall form it resembles 14th-century gatehouses at Carlisle, Alnwick and Prudhoe and its details compare with local castles such as Belsay, Chipchase and Hylton.

After the suppression of the priory, the castle passed under the control of a constable or governor. The governor and officials of the castle lived in the gatehouse and an inventory of 1585 lists the furnishings of those domestic interiors. The brightly coloured cloth hangings mentioned in the inventory perhaps came from cargo on ships in the harbour, for in 1575 the bailey [bailiff] of North Shields boarded every ship in the haven at the castle and 'did take up, for the furnytur of her majestie's castle, whatsoever she had in lodinge, a parcel of everything for the service of the castle at the queen's majestie's price'.

Above: Tynemouth gatehouse, with its barbican in the foreground. Note how the gatehouse has lost both its angle turrets and the projecting parapet from the barbican since 1780

History

The headland at Tynemouth has a long and varied history spanning nearly two millennia. Today, the priory headland has a windswept beauty which makes it difficult to imagine that until the 1950s it housed a garrison, the last in a series of communities to have lived here that stretches back to the Iron Age.

EARLY HISTORY AND THE SAXON MONASTERY

Archaeological excavations following the demolition of army buildings north of the Priory church in 1960 uncovered the remains of circular wooden huts, some probably pre-dating the Roman occupation and others from the second century AD. They are the earliest evidence for occupation on the headland and are thought to have been inhabited by the Votadini tribe, an Iron-Age people. The Roman fort of Arbeia lay across the river in South Shields, on the hill now called the Lawe.

The modern history of Tynemouth begins with the foundation of a monastery on the headland: it is not known exactly when it was established, but it is likely that it was founded by or with the protection of the Anglian Kings of Northumbria, a kingdom which stretched from the Humber to the Forth. It was thus one of a small group of monasteries, together with Lindisfarne, Jarrow, Wearmouth and Whitby, which helped to spread Christianity through the North. For the Venerable Bede (c.673–735), a monk at the nearby monastery of Jarrow, who wrote the *Ecclesiastical History of the English People*, the first ever history of the English, the mouth of the river Tyne was where the great missionary St Cuthbert (635–87) performed a miracle in his youth, saving a group of monks from drowning. According to Bede, their monastery was situated at the river mouth but probably on the south bank, while Tynemouth headland appears to have been unoccupied. By 792, however, the house existed and was sufficiently important to be chosen as the burial place that year for King Osred II of Northumbria. The Saxon monastery suffered terribly from Viking raids in the ninth century: in 875 it might have been destroyed and the site briefly occupied by the invaders.

NORMAN TYNEMOUTH

After the destruction of the monastery, Tynemouth is not documented again until the mid-11th century. Tostig, earl of Northumberland (d.1066) was entertained several times here. On one occasion his chaplain lodged in 'the tower of the parish church of St Mary', proof that a church stood as part of the settlement here.

It was in this building in 1065 that the body of the future patron saint of Tynemouth, King Oswine (644–651), was said to have been discovered. Oswine was a Christian king of Deira (the southern part of Northumbria approximating to modern Yorkshire), who according to Bede was famed for his goodness, but was driven from his throne and murdered by a rival at 'Ingentlingum', probably Gilling West (Yorkshire) in 651.

Although there is no early tradition linking Oswine to Tynemouth, the story that his remains were found there was believed and the saint has forever afterwards been linked to

Above: *Page from a psalter, with interlace initial, damaged by fire. An inscription recorded that this book belonged to the seventh-century St Oswine, buried at Tynemouth. This is not possible, as the psalter was made in Ireland in the 11th century, but it could have belonged to Tynemouth Priory and been associated with St Oswine's relics or tomb*

this headland. There are two conflicting descriptions of the discovery. The first appears in a 12th-century Life of St Oswine, which explains that Oswine appeared in a dream to the parish priest and revealed his burial place. With the help of the bishop of Durham a successful search was made for the body, which proved to be fresh and sweet-smelling. It was washed, clothed and placed in a shrine. The alternative account of the discovery is that Oswine's body was found by Ælfred Westou, a monk of Durham who was an enthusiastic and suspiciously successful relic collector.

Soon after this discovery, the church at Tynemouth was again destroyed. After his victory at the battle of Hastings in 1066, William the Conqueror was crowned king of England. The north of England offered resistance to Norman rule and during the devastation that followed, Tynemouth was destroyed. In 1074, a monk called Alduin, inspired by Bede's description of the great religious houses of Northumbria, set out from the Cotswolds with two others to re-establish a monastery at Jarrow. Their community flourished and soon afterwards, Waltheof, last English earl of Northumberland, granted the church of St Mary at Tynemouth, with the body of St Oswine, and all the lands belonging to it, to Alduin and the monks at Jarrow. In this period, the headland was not permanently occupied and Oswine's bones were regularly carried by the new community from Tynemouth to Jarrow. In 1083 a small community was installed at Tynemouth under a monk called Turchil, who re-roofed the ruined church.

Below: Monks translating the relics of two saints in procession, 14th century. During the translation of St Oswine's relics at Tynemouth the saint was credited with saving a visitor's horse from falling to its death down the cliff

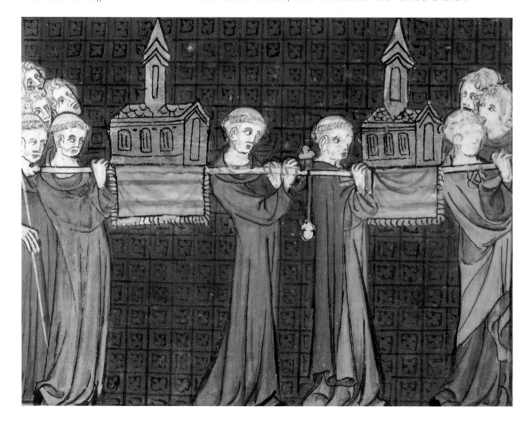

MONASTERY AND STRONGHOLD

Turchil and his companions were not left in possession of Tynemouth for long. King William II Rufus installed Robert de Mowbray, one of the most powerful of his supporters, as earl of Northumberland in about 1090. The Jarrow monks, and by extension Turchil and his companions, had since 1083 fallen under the jurisdiction of Durham Cathedral. When the new earl quarrelled with the bishop of Durham, the earl ejected the monks at Tynemouth and gave the monastery to the great Benedictine Abbey of St Albans, Hertfordshire with a generous endowment of land. The monks were furious and regarded the death of the abbot of St Albans in 1093 as a divine judgement on this bequest. For the rest of its history — despite its wealth and several unsuccessful attempts to assert its independence — Tynemouth was subject to the authority of St Albans. Consequently Tynemouth was a priory, the governing officer or prior being subservient to the abbot of St Albans, its mother house.

In 1095, Earl Robert revolted against William Rufus. The king and a royal army marched north to besiege his principal strongholds. The earl and 30 followers took refuge in Tynemouth, where they held out for six days. Robert was wounded in the leg and tried to take sanctuary in the church, but was dragged out. After a long imprisonment he reputedly became a monk of St Albans. The curious dual character of Tynemouth in the events of 1095 as both a stronghold and monastery was to persist right through the Middle Ages.

During the 1090s work began on a new set of monastic buildings at Tynemouth. The first stage was the construction of a church jointly dedicated to St Oswine and the Virgin Mary. This building was sufficiently complete to receive the body of Malcolm III, king of Scotland, after his death in battle at the hands of Earl Robert in 1093. It was not until 20 August 1110 that the remains of St Oswine were ceremoniously transferred to the new church. This ceremony probably marked the completion of the east end of the church.

ST OSWINE

A year later, an anonymous monk of St Albans composed a Life of St Oswine which records his numerous miracles. During the translation ceremony in 1110, for example, a visitor's tethered horse was saved from falling to its death down the cliff by the intercession of St Oswine. The list of miracles in the Life continued to be updated until the late 12th century and the events they record help chart the development of the monastic complex. In 1111 a man called Arkill fell from the roof of the church (work possibly continued to the nave after the translation ceremony). By the intercession of Oswine he recovered, only to fall again 19 feet from the dormitory during work to that building. Thanks to St Oswine, however, he only sprained his foot.

Above: Stained-glass window from York Minster, depicting a man falling off a ladder. St Oswine was credited with many miracles — among them that of saving Arkill from two falls from the church roof and the dormitory in 1111 — he escaped with a light sprain

Above: Goldsmith at his furnace. Baldwin, a famous goldsmith from St Albans worked on St Oswine's shrine in the 1190s. It is said that when metal from his workshop was stolen, the thief was captured by the saint's intervention

The description of a fire in about 1150, reveals that the dormitory, refectory and guesthouse were all thatched. Monks climbed up to extinguish the flames, while others removed valuables from the church. The prior himself carried Oswine's shrine to the safety of the grassed cloister and begged the saint to extinguish the flames, which were then seen to die down.

In 1174 the long-running quarrel between St Albans and Durham for the control of Tynemouth was settled in favour of St Albans. The monastery entered a period of prosperity and secured important concessions for trade, taxation and the exercise of law within its estates. Particularly important in this respect was a grant of King Richard I in 1189 that constituted the monastic estates as the 'Liberty of Tynemouth' under the direct control of St Oswine and the priory.

These changes were accompanied by a redevelopment of the monastery. Most important was the building of a sumptuous new east end of the church as a setting for the shrine of St Oswine. To judge from its surviving architectural details, work to this building probably began in about 1190. It was probably also accompanied by alterations to the shrine of Oswine undertaken by a celebrated goldsmith from St Albans called Baldwin. His presence at Tynemouth is documented because St Oswine was credited with bringing about the capture of a thief who stole metal from his workshop.

In about 1220–50, the nave was lengthened and provided with a new west front. Other works to the cloister buildings followed in the 1250s and 1260s, including the repair of windows in the refectory. It was probably in this period that the chapter house was remodelled in its present form.

ECONOMIC AND POLITICAL RIVALRIES

There was continuous economic rivalry between the town of Newcastle and Tynemouth Priory. Like many monasteries, Tynemouth tried to increase its wealth through commerce. Its development of the port of North Shields threatened the economic monopolies in the trade of coal, wool and fish which the powerful town of Newcastle claimed along the whole river downstream to the sea. These commodities were widely exported in Britain and Europe. In 1270 the mayor of Newcastle led an armed force and burned down North Shields, and by 1290 Newcastle successfully petitioned the king to suspend trade from the new settlement.

At the same time, Tynemouth's attempts to gain independence from St Albans Abbey were thwarted when St Albans and Newcastle banded together to persuade the king that Tynemouth's activities were an infringement of royal authority. The campaign culminated in the forfeiture of the Liberty of Tynemouth. Despite appeals to the king, St Albans won the day and in 1294 the abbot made a midnight raid on the priory, arresting the rebellious prior and his accomplices.

EDWARD I AND THE SCOTTISH WARS

King Edward I's attempt to arbitrate in the succession of the Scottish crown plunged the border into prolonged and bitter warfare. In 1296 Tynemouth received a royal licence to erect fortifications and the headland became an important stronghold under the control of the prior. These fortifications, enclosing the priory buildings, made the headland into a castle-like stronghold. The war brought one unexpected advantage. Edward I visited the priory regularly and had a private oratory erected for his use. His queen, Margaret, also stayed here between June and October 1303 and again in 1304. This hospitality gave the community the opportunity to petition for the restoration of several privileges lost in 1292. During this last visit, the queen's trumpeter was robbed of his silver and gilt trumpets by the inhabitants of Tynemouth.

In 1312 Edward I's son and successor, Edward II, arrived at Tynemouth with his unpopular favourite Piers Gaveston as a fugitive from a powerful alliance of hostile nobles. The king took a ship from the headland despite heavy seas and the pleas of his wife, Isabella, who was heavily pregnant. Soon afterwards the king and Gaveston were captured and the royal favourite brutally executed. A bastard son of Edward II, called Adam, was also buried at Tynemouth in 1322.

When the English were defeated at Bannockburn in 1314, government in parts of northern England broke down. The prior, Richard de Tewing, attempted to protect the monastery, clearing houses from around the gatehouse and paying for a garrison of 80 men. In 1318, the king appointed a custodian of priory fortifications, recognition that the headland was a stronghold of outstanding importance.

Left: A fair blessed by a bishop, 14th century. Tynemouth Priory and Newcastle became bitter economic rivals when the priory developed North Shields, threatening Newcastle's trade in coal, wool and fish

THE MONASTERY PROSPERS

Although the war put a heavy strain on monastic resources, the priory buildings continued to develop with the re-roofing of the 'monks' houses' in 1320 and the completion of the Lady Chapel by 1336 under Prior Tewing. His successor, Prior Thomas de la Mare, was also a capable leader, thwarting an attempt by the king's governor of the border, the warden of the march, to claim control of the headland as a royal castle, and spending more that £800 on the priory buildings. This included moving the shrine of St Oswine to a new location, possibly in the Lady Chapel.

In the face of renewed hostilities with Scotland, Richard II pledged the substantial sum of 500 marks to the priory for desperate repairs to the defences in February 1390, while two of the most powerful men in the region, John of Gaunt, duke of Lancaster, and Henry Percy, earl of Northumberland,

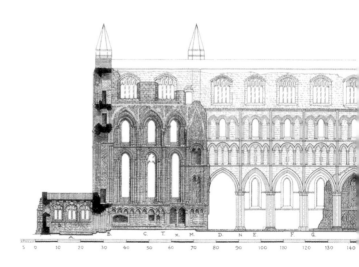

also made grants. This money was used to construct the great gatehouse that still serves as the entrance to the headland.

Over the 15th century the priory prospered. In 1462, Queen Margaret of Anjou made an unsuccessful landing at Tynemouth as part of a bid to spark off a popular rising in the North in favour of her dethroned husband, King Henry VI. Soon afterwards, and possibly as part of an attempt to secure the priory's future loyalty, his rival for the throne, King Edward IV, confirmed the 1189 charter issued by Richard I, with its extensive benefits. The prior who secured this grant was John Langton, who probably erected the so-called Percy Chantry at the east end of the church (see pages 8–10). It was presumably built before Langton was deposed in 1478 as part of a complex triangle of intrigue connecting Tynemouth, St Albans and Binham, Norfolk, another of its rich cells.

SIXTEENTH CENTURY AND SUPPRESSION

As a rich and powerful monastery, Tynemouth was now an attractive prize for those in search of church preferment. The priors appointed in the early 16th century were well connected at court. One of these, Prior Stonewell, even secured independence from St Albans through the agency of Thomas Wolsey, the celebrated minister of Henry VIII. His successor, Thomas Gardiner, was a former chaplain to the king. A final impression of the physical condition of the medieval priory is provided by a survey of 1527. This describes the castle walls, barns and granaries, glass windows and the lead on the church roof all in need of repair.

Early in 1536, as a prelude to his assault on the wealth of the Church, Henry VIII's commissioners brought serious but unsubstantiated charges of misconduct against the prior and 7 of the 15 monks at Tynemouth. Three years later, on 12 January 1539, Prior Blakeney and his community signed the

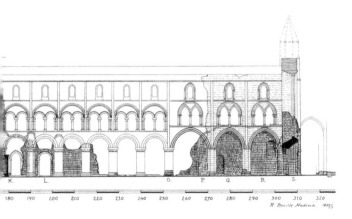

Left: Tynemouth priory section. The parts that survive are shaded. Taken from Archaeologia Aeliana series 4 Volume XIV (1937)

Right: *Plan of Tynemouth Castle in
1545, possibly by Gian Tommaso
Scala, an Italian fortifications expert
and advisor to Henry VIII. The design
shows new defences for both the
river and the approach by land. Two
massive arrow-headed gun
platforms (bastions), new in England
at the time, were to be connected
by a curtain wall and ditch. New
defences were constructed, but the
bastions were never built*

deed which surrendered Tynemouth monastery, and all
its possessions, to the king. The monks received pensions
and goods, stores and farm stock were sold; Henry's
commissioners took away the church bells and the gold and
silver. St Oswine's shrine was broken up; his bones scattered.
It was the end of monastic life at Tynemouth.

THE TUDOR DEFENCES

When Henry VIII's commissioners took over the priory in
1539, its buildings were quickly turned to defensive use to
control the entrance to the Tyne. The first major works took
place in the 1540s when Henry VIII was faced with an alliance
between Spain and France and the prospect of an invasion. In
1544, alarmed at rumours of French plans to land forces in
the North and in Scotland, Henry sent a fleet and army to
the Tyne under the command of the earl of Hertford. The
headland was made into a military camp and supply base,
while engineers led by Sir Richard Lee surveyed and planned
improvements to fortresses in the border country. A plan for
the new fortifications, from 1545, was probably the work of
Gian Tommaso Scala, an Italian military adviser working with
Lee who used Italian design principles that were new to
England. The strategic problem at Tynemouth was that the
headland did not entirely command the river mouth. Their
solution was to create a new line of fortification, west of the

The Black Middens

In 1582 the mayor of Newcastle was instructed to arrange for 'a continual light in the night season in the east end of the church of Tynemouth Castle' to safeguard passing ships. This order probably revived an old monastic practice of maintaining a brazier to guide vessels safely past the jagged rocks called the Black Middens beyond the headland.

The staircase that gave access to the east end of the church collapsed in 1659 and alternative arrangements for the light had to be made. By 1664, the governor of the castle had built a lighthouse on the headland which was replaced in 1775. From 1802 the lighthouse burnt an oil lamp rather than coal and contained silver-plated reflectors and a revolving mechanism. The cost was met by a tax that ships paid to the Custom House at Newcastle Quay. When the lighthouse was demolished in 1898, 200 carved medieval stones were found in its structure. A safe channel to the river was marked in 1536 by High and Low Lights at North Shields, rebuilt in 1711 and 1808.

Despite the lighthouses, ships were often blown onto the Black Middens. When SS *Stanley* went down in 1864, the life-saving apparatus, a seat slung from a rope wound in from the shore, jammed and all 24 people on board were drowned. Soon after a volunteer Life Brigade was formed, the first in the country. It introduced rocket-fired lines to throw ropes to people on wrecked ships. The timber-clad Life Brigade building of 1886–7 by C T Gomoszynski, facing the Spanish Battery, is now a museum and is still the headquarters for the volunteers. By 1895 the piers sheltered the harbour and reduced the dangers, but ships still ran aground, and the volunteers saved many lives.

Despite the lighthouses, ships were often blown onto the Black Middens, jagged rocks submerged at high tide

Below: The Lifeboat off Tynemouth Bay, by Edward Duncan (1803–82)

Above: Sir Arthur Hesilrige
(1601–61) by an unknown artist.
Hesilrige captured Tynemouth for
Parliament in 1648

castle walls, which enclosed the priory and the headland to its south, with Prior's Haven in between.

The principal features of Scala's plan were two massive angle bastions, arrowhead-shaped gun platforms that projected to landward from each end of a curtain wall and wide ditch. These were to provide offensive fire to protect the landward approaches and defensive fire along the curtain, allowing guns inside the fortress to control the river mouth. Had the whole scheme been completed, it would have been the first use of the angle bastion in England. A plan of Tynemouth drawn in the 1580s (see page 12) reveals what was completed; the curtain wall and ditch, with some flanking positions along it but not full bastions as planned. The lower headland, which was to have been the site of one angle bastion, had an artillery position which became known as Spanish Battery. In later times it was a key element of the fortifications but its distance from the barracks in the castle and priory was a constant source of irritation to the gunners.

THE CIVIL WAR

In common with many English coastal defences when imminent threat subsided, those built at Tynemouth in the 16th century were subsequently neglected, though a small garrison was maintained and a fine survey plan of the castle was produced in 1582 during a foreign invasion scare. Tynemouth's defences were not tested until the 1640s, and the Civil War between king and Parliament. Newcastle and Bristol were the only two large ports which remained loyal to the king, able to resupply his army and deny vital coal supplies to London and the parliamentarians. Newcastle was heavily fortified, as was Tynemouth, notably at Spanish Battery where the ramparts were heightened in brick and provided with casemates for heavy guns. The castle was also well equipped with 29 guns and 500 muskets, but suffered, like Newcastle, from an outbreak of plague. Eight soldiers died in a week, 60 others were ill, as well as the chief surgeon.

Newcastle remained with the king until shortly after the collapse of royalist forces in the North after the battle of Marston Moor on 2 July 1644, and was taken by Scots forces fighting for Parliament in October of that year. For a short time in 1648, however, the garrison once more declared for the king. Sir Arthur Hesilrige, the parliamentary commander in Newcastle, responded with a swift night attack. It was a spectacular success, with only three parliamentarian soldiers wounded and one killed. Its economic importance was commemorated in a pamphlet in praise of Hesilrige which declared 'Let London especially remember this, for unlesse so happily regained, no more coles could be expected this year.' There could be no clearer reference to the importance of coal exported from Newcastle at the time.

GUNS AND GARRISON

The Tynemouth defences remained important during the rest
of the 17th century. During the First Dutch War of 1652–4
the garrison comprised a master gunner and 20 gunners with
seven guns, and a small infantry detachment. In the 1660s, the
governor Colonel Edward Villiers built new barracks, a
lighthouse and a house for himself using stone from the
priory. He paid Robert Trollope, who worked on his house
and lighthouse (and on the new parish church), £40 for
repairs in 1675, including a new floor over the church for
a magazine.

The Tyne was further secured from 1672 when Clifford's
Fort was built on the river banks a little upstream towards
North Shields. This fort was the main defence of the river
through the 18th century, though batteries were maintained in
the castle, at Spanish Battery and in South Shields on the
south bank of the Tyne. In the 1750s a battery of six guns in
the castle served to defend ships at anchor in the approaches.

There was always a small infantry garrison at Tynemouth
and during the 18th century a master gunner, with a few
regulars, maintained guns on the headland, Spanish Battery
and Clifford's Fort. Local militia, sailors and volunteers joined
them during the Jacobite rebellions in 1715 and 1745, the
Seven Years' War of 1756–63, the American war of 1776–83
and the French Revolutionary and Napoleonic wars of
1793–1815. In March 1758, the Board of Ordnance built new

*Below: In 1810, during the
Napoleonic wars, the Percy Chantry
was used as a powder magazine. In
1850 it was given back to the
parish and restored by the
Newcastle architect John Dobson*

Top: The Tyne at North Shields in about 1895, busy with shipping, both sail and steam. Note High and Low Lights on the right.
Above: *Guiseppe Garibaldi (1807–82), Italian national hero, sailed in 1854 from Baltimore into Tynemouth where he was greeted enthusiastically and presented with a sword. He stayed on Tyneside for a month*

gun batteries in Tynemouth, and temporary barracks for 1,000 men, possibly where Knott Flats are now, as there was not enough room in the castle. During the 1780s Captain E Durnford adapted the castle gatehouse as a barracks. A small detachment of regulars from a Royal Artillery marching company maintained the guns, by 1795 numbering an officer and 11 men. The county militia assisted as did, from 1797, the local Tynemouth Volunteer Artillery. By 1805 all the Tynemouth batteries had a formidable armament of heavy guns comprising 32 18-pounder guns, eight 12-pounders and 11 9-pounders.

A MODERN COASTAL FORTRESS

When the Napoleonic wars ended in 1815 coastal defence was reduced. In 1824, a master gunner and one assistant maintained the Tynemouth guns. By the late 1840s, fear of the imperial intentions of France re-emerged. The introduction of new steam-powered ironclad warships (the first was the French *La Gloire* in 1860), and the invention of more accurate and devastating rifled guns, exposed Britain's ageing and run-down defences. A massive programme of fortress building in the 1860s and 1870s, particularly around the major naval bases, largely bypassed Tynemouth, although by 1881 it had been given six modern rifled guns.

The transformation of Tynemouth into a modern coastal fortress came in the last 20 years of the 19th century, as the threat from France receded and gave way to a new one, Germany, whose growing naval forces posed a direct threat to Scotland and the North. In 1882 Lord Morley's government committee recognized the need to protect the main northern mercantile ports on the Forth and the Tyne and recommended four breech-loading (BL) guns at Tynemouth to protect coal exports, the Armstrong armaments factories at Elswick, and the extensive shipyards. Today, among green river banks and newly built houses, it is hard to imagine the vanished industrial riverside of shipyards, coal staithes, collieries and factories.

In 1888 a submarine minefield was laid to protect the river mouth. This was a system of tethered mines either floating or at set depths, which could be detonated electrically by cables run from a control post on shore to sink hostile ships. A special unit, the Tyne Division Royal Engineers (Volunteers) Submarine Miners, operated from Clifford's Fort, where some of their red-brick buildings survive. In 1891, work on two powerful 6-inch BL guns began and gun mountings were improved soon after. By 1905 Tynemouth headland had a modern armament of two 6-inch guns, two 12-pounder quick-firing (QF) guns, and one 9.2-inch gun, while Spanish Battery had two 6-inch and two 12-pounder QF guns.

By the early 1900s, target data acquired from range- and position-finding instruments in small buildings on and off site could be relayed electrically to a Fire Command Post on the headland which allocated targets to the guns where range and bearing appeared on clock dials. The 12-pounder QF guns were targeted more quickly using optical autosights on the guns.

This powerful armament gave defence at both long and close range, supported by new buildings for fire command and range-finding, searchlights to illuminate the harbour mouth

Above: Harriet Martineau (1802–76) in 1849 by George Richmond. The writer and journalist lived in rented rooms in Tynemouth during a period of debilitating illness during the 1840s

Below: *Significant features guarding the mouth of the River Tyne from Roman times to the 20th century*

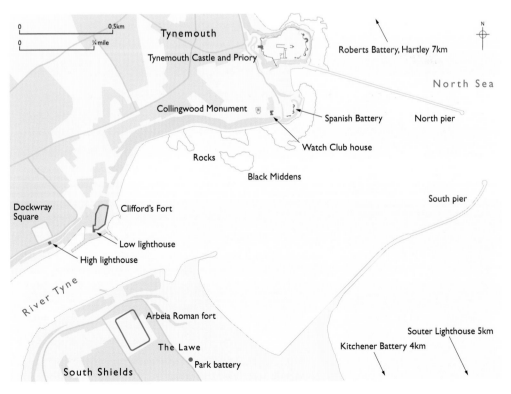

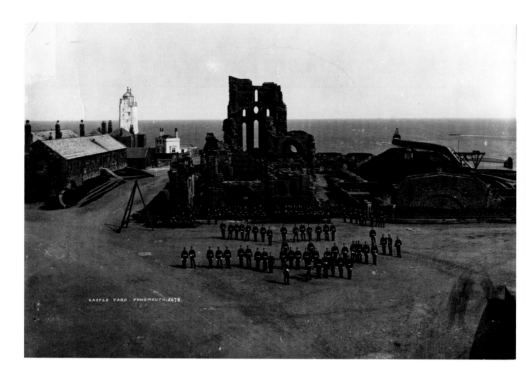

Above: *Castle Yard, Tynemouth in about 1895. Note the ammunition magazine to the centre right of the priory where the former monastic buildings are now laid out, and also the barracks, governor's house and lighthouse to the left of the picture – all now gone*

at night and new barracks and facilities for the garrison. By the outbreak of the First World War in 1914, the headland had become the centre of a large and integrated Fire Command, based in a building now demolished (on the site of the Coastguard Station), controlling all gun batteries along an area of the coast north to Blyth and south to Sunderland.

THE FIRST WORLD WAR

On the eve of the First World War, the Tyne was producing one third of the country's naval ships. The Admiralty recognized that its shipbuilding yards and ordnance factories ran a close second in importance to the principal naval bases at Portsmouth and Plymouth. Naval flotillas patrolled the North Sea and the ageing battleship HMS *Illustrious* was sent to guard the Tyne. German warships eluded the Royal Navy only once. In December 1914, they bombarded Hartlepool, Whitby and Scarborough, causing great damage and loss of life. As a consequence, the defences of Tynemouth Fire Command were strengthened by the construction between 1917 and 1921 of two 12-inch gun turrets using surplus guns from HMS *Illustrious*; one to the north at Roberts Battery, Hartley, the other to the south at Kitchener Battery, Marsden. These were big guns capable of engaging battleships far out at sea. They received target data from a seven-storey rangefinding tower (behind Percy Gardens) which worked with the Fire Command Post on the headland.

The minefield was maintained at the river mouth and, to counteract the new Zeppelin threat, anti-aircraft guns and searchlights were installed on open spaces, although no Zeppelins in fact managed to attack Tynemouth.

A Ship is Mined

Arthur Lloyd served as a gunner and then an optical range finder at Tynemouth from 1940 to 1943. He recalls watching a Dutch ship hit a mine off Tynemouth in August 1941.

'It was awful to see but the worst for me was that I was on duty and was looking down into the harbour, just up the north pier. It was 31 August 1941 and a small Dutch coasting vessel of a reasonable size was coming up the Tyne on its way down south to London. It was carrying a load of copper. It was just down below the castle by the north pier, sailing up, and I was on the gun. I was puzzled because it had coloured flags up and down the mast to port and stern and I thought that was unusual as they only flew flags as a code to enter the port. I found out later that it was named after the river Marne and that the Dutch crew had put the flags up for their Queen Wilhelmina's birthday.

'I could see men on deck doing various jobs. All of a sudden, there was a tremendous explosion. The ship had hit an acoustic or magnetic mine. It was like a dull roar and the sea rose up as high as a house and and I watched in horror as everything disappeared and all the water came down again like a huge waterfall. I just caught sight of the stern disappearing. Eleven men were killed and they all disappeared without trace. Then dozens of seagulls appeared squawking round and picking up things. I was horrified, saddened.'

Above: Arthur Lloyd in January 1941, aged 22, with a Bren gun in the Prior's Haven
Below: The tanker British Officer sinks off Tynemouth on 1 December 1940 having hit a mine. Fifteen of her 47-man crew were killed

Above: Waves crashing over North Pier, with the ruins of Tynemouth Priory in the foreground

1920S TO THE PRESENT DAY

After the end of the war in 1918, the guns of Tynemouth Fire Command were put into a state of care and maintenance, and from 1922 only the headland's 9.2-inch and 6-inch guns continued in use for training.

When war came in 1939, the Fire Command was reactivated and evolved a sophisticated system of centralized control, made more efficient by the introduction of radar to gunnery by 1942. The headland had one 9.2-inch BL gun for counter-bombardment defence against distant enemy ships, and two 6-inch guns for closer defence.

Towards the end of the war, the Tynemouth batteries were manned increasingly by the Home Guard and, after the war, by the Territorial Army. By 1952 the 9.2-inch gun was in care and maintenance, with only the 6-inch guns providing active defence. In 1956 coast artillery was disbanded. The nation's defences now relied on the new guided rockets, and all the Tynemouth Fire Command's fixed guns were scrapped.

The military buildings at Tynemouth, including the barracks and governor's house, parts of which dated to the 17th century, were almost entirely demolished in 1960 in an attempt to clear the headland of post-medieval features: something that probably would not happen today. The coastal batteries were not so easily destroyed and survived to be restored by English Heritage. A 6-inch Mk XXXIII gun was emplaced in 1993 by English Heritage, assisted by 101 Regiment RA (V.), the Tynemouth Volunteer Artillery Association, and the Fortress Study Group, as a symbol of Tynemouth's role in the defence of the north-east coast.